101 THINGS
JESUS NEVER SAID

F44/12

Also available from Marshall Pickering

SNOGGING
Simon Mayo & Martin Wroe

101 THINGS
JESUS NEVER SAID
...and quite a bit more besides

**MARTIN WROE, ADRIAN REITH
AND SIMON PARKE**

Cartoons by Nick Newman

Marshall Pickering
An Imprint of HarperCollins*Publishers*

Marshall Pickering is an Imprint of
HarperCollins*Religious*
Part of HarperCollins*Publishers*
77–85 Fulham Palace Road, London W6 8JB

First published in Great Britain
in 1992 by Marshall Pickering

1 3 5 7 9 10 8 6 4 2

Text copyright © 1992
Martin Wroe, Adrian Reith and Simon Parke
Illustrations copyright © 1992 Nick Newman

A catalogue record for this book is
available from the British Library

ISBN 0 551 02694 4

Printed and bound in Great Britain by
HarperCollinsManufacturing Glasgow

CONTENTS

INTRODUCTION

===

It is reckoned that the public ministry of Jesus lasted only three years, before things got altogether too threatening for the powers-that-were – who promptly had a natter and then murdered him by nailing him to some wood. And why not? We all have to do something with our unacknowledged fears, and crucifying people is certainly one way of letting off steam.

So that was Jesus's lot. Or rather, his "little". Because three years isn't very long at all really – especially if you're a contender in the "Great Historical Figure" category. After all, pause for a moment and reflect on some of the dinosaurs who've lumbered around the world stage so unimpressively this century (no names, no pack drill). Few have been in the public eye for anything like such a short time as Jesus – James Dean, Marilyn Monroe, Jimmy Osmond. And Jesus had no access to the media.

Hang it all – we're even surprising ourselves as we write these lines. Here is a public life which could

IN THE BEGINNING

have been fitted in comfortably between Olympic Games, World Cup Finals *and* General Elections – with a year or two to spare. While 2.3 public ministries of Jesus could have been squeezed into the training course of an architect (mmm . . .). Yet here we are, still discussing him in pubs, on buses, in newspapers, on the radio – and even in church occasionally. Some even *worship* him. About a billion at the last count. It must have been the way he told them.

The main interest of this book, however, is in the opposite direction. It is in the way he didn't tell 'em. Our interest is in the things he *didn't* say. And the choice, of course, is mind-boggling. Yes, for the sheer brevity of his public ministry gave him ample opportunity *not* to say vast numbers of things; enormous scope *not* to have a wide variety of conversations; large amounts of time *not* to express an opinion on many and various topics.

Now for some this is not a problem. For those who think the garden of life could actually do with a few less fences – just more respect for that which is beautiful and precious – the brevity of this public life and consequent absence of explicit instruction, is startling, but no problem. For others, though, it is. It's a major problem. For the Fence-Erectors, the minimally reported three years definitely needs a good deal of touching up to ensure no loopholes. For the Faith-

Defectors, on the other hand, it needs toning down, domesticating, putting into perspective, etc. Thus an unholy and unlikely alliance is formed, agreed only in the desire for disinformation.

And the result? Simple. Devastatingly simple. The quiet rewriting of history. If Jesus didn't say something, it doesn't matter. We won't panic. We'll just pretend he did. So we take a few of our own half-baked, home-spun, cock-eyed ideas – and hang them on him; lay them on his lips. Or somewhere near them at least. That way, Jesus, like Marmite, can be for each of us, "my mate". We agree with him completely – because we're the ventriloquist and he's the dummy. "Gottle of gear, gottle of gear." "Precisely Jesus – that's just what *I* was saying!"

It's all absolutely marvellous, really. Because once you get the hang of it, you can not only invent things he said ("Time's a great healer"), you can also invent things he did ("Walking in England's green and pleasant land"), and attitudes he adopted ("Really each partner should have at least one foot on the floor in all cases of intimacy before marriage"). A regular roller-coaster of invention, and prejudices confirmed for at least one more night of our brief stay on this planet. . . .

101 Things Jesus Never Said is an attempt at path-clearing. It is an inadequate attempt by a flawed,

NEAR THE END OF THE BEGINNING

fallible and foolish trio whose only real reward is the faint hope of a handsome royalty cheque in the distant future. Unless of course, there is a still more glorious reward and our Lord returns first.

THE END OF THE BEGINNING

1

God helps those who help themselves.
Er, yes . . . what about those who are helpless?

2

God is a Man

Now, he never said that. Not once. Not ever, never,
never. So why on earth (they don't do it in Heaven)
does almost everyone think God is male? Sure, he
said stuff like "Our Father", and described God as a
King, but he also talked of God like a mother, like
a hen with her chicks, and in the Old Testament,
which Jesus knew like the back of his hand, God
even gets called "the breasted one". And they
weren't thinking of sumo wrestlers either.

'Course, Jesus was a man, and most Christians
believe that Jesus was God, and so maybe they
figure that two and two, er, makes God a Man too.
But if God was turning up on earth as a human
being, well there were only two possibilities. He
probably got Gabriel to flip a coin for it, and you
can't base your theology of the sexuality of God on
something as chancy as flipping a coin, can you?
Not even one flipped somewhere where they
actually claim to understand the doctrine of
Predestination.

3

DISCIPLE: You taught us to say "Our Father".
JESUS: Indeed I did.
DISCIPLE: So what is he like – this "Father"?
JESUS: What's he like? Well, how can I put it?
I suppose he is the "uncaused cause", basically. The imminent yet transcendent "is-ness", amidst, yet at the same time beyond, the universe. He's the intrinsically unknowable ground of reality – in a word, the "mysterium tremendum".
DISCIPLE: Oh. I see.

4

Thunderbolts and lightning, very, very frightening
. . . God
Actually, that's an adapted line from a song by the popular music group Queen. But there is a strongly held view among some that God is out to get everyone, that he's going to stretch out his hairy hand and zap us with a lightning bolt of cosmic proportions. For example, even clergymen who speak out of turn could find their house burned down – House of God notwithstanding. In fact, although Jesus didn't have a treacly, sweetie-pie view of the

GOD

Almighty, he didn't portray him as an eternal sadist either, spending his days having a whale of a time getting people to slip up on banana skins, sending thunderbolts down their chimneys, afflicting them with strange diseases or aimlessly snuffing out the life in their loved ones.

Nowhere does Jesus give the impression that God is some fierce, bad-tempered old buffer, getting his thrills from zapping his earthly friends with vicious tortures.

Trouble is, you wouldn't believe that, given some people's views these days, like those churchmen who thought that a lightning bolt on York Cathedral, causing hundreds of thousands of pounds' damage to an historic building, was God's way of getting back at the Bishop of Durham for saying he wasn't so certain about the Virgin Birth or the resurrection business.

Is God really that petty?

Is he really that bad a shot? Durham Cathedral is hundreds of miles north of York.

5

Did I ever tell you that I'm going to be David Icke in a later life?

DAVID ICKE

14

6

*God? He's up in Heaven, floating around on a cloud,
that long white beard of his trailing over the edge
while he dozes.*

Odd as it may seem, given the tendency of
contemporary cartoonists to depict the Almighty
sitting on some puffy, fluffy clouds surrounded by
cherubs plucking harps, these images do not have
their historical root in the words of Jesus, who, er,
ought to know about these things, claiming as he
did to be on close family terms with the Supreme
Being.

Does Jesus anywhere give the impression that
God is some daft old buffer with snowy facial growth
who can't remember what day it is – let alone what
time it is or even, come to think of it, what universe
he's in today? Er, no.

There does seem to be a touch of artistic cross-
fertilization here between Father Christmas, Old
Father Time, Captain Birdseye and . . . God. All we
can tell from Jesus's words about the person he
called his Father is . . . well, not much really, when
it comes to distinguishing physical features, scars,
inside leg measurement and how many sugars he
takes in his tea.

GOD

Jesus seemed more interested in describing how God behaves rather than what he looks like. Throwing big meals for the homeless, welcoming home ungrateful children, paying a day's wages to people who've only worked for ten minutes before closing time . . . that sort of thing. Get the picture? Pretty strange, eh?

7

God's a nice old boy really, he knows what we're like. Between you and me, he'll let anything pass . . . Er, yes, well interesting, in fact *common*, idea, but again not really one found in what Jesus had to say on the subject. It's true that his big thing was how much in love with everyone God is, how he's completely passionate about every single person, totally devoted to their well-being, almost infatuated . . . but unfortunately that's not all there is on the business.

Jesus does have a bit of awkward stuff about judgement and behaving oneself and, er, generally trying to live a good life – you know, fairly straightforward stuff like, well, like this: "Be ye therefore perfect as your Father in Heaven is perfect."

GOD

Hmmm. Not that he expected perfection all at once of course. Just that we should have a proper go. We should give it a try. That was the general idea in the first place.

8

Give God a chance, you might get to like the old chap. He's not so bad.

Well, yes, it's true that he's not so bad. In fact he's not at all bad – it's not allowed for God to be bad. You actually get disqualified from being God if you're bad.

So God's quite good actually but this kind of approach is a bit on the low-key side for Jesus, a touch lackadaisical shall we say. Jesus was a bit more upfront about it all, a bit firmer. You know – "You shall love the Lord your God with all your heart and all your soul and all your mind. This is the first and great commandment." That sort of thing.

9

There is a God-shaped gap in every person's life.
Common line in all the best evangelistic sermons, but utter drivel in fact. You can't fit God in a gap. It would be like trying to fit the universe in your ear. It's people who are supposed to be God-shaped, not gaps.

UTTER DRIVEL

10

Earn all you can, save all you can, give all you can.
Sounds more like John Wesley actually.

11

God is a Woman.
Some ancient religions had female gods, true, and it
is within the female species that new life begins
and is nurtured and eventually born. (But you
probably already knew that.) Then there's the
Blessed Virgin Mary, the Mother of God – now she
was a woman. But that's about it. Still, if you have
to choose God's gender, you should probably plump
for woman – just to try to get a balance after all
these centuries of "him" being male. A couple of
millennia of *Our Mother in Heaven* would probably
balance the history of Christian theology out a bit.

12

Thank God it's Friday.

BLESSED VIRGIN MARY

13

*God is An Interesting Concept but Not Actually
There in Reality, in a Very Real Sense. Or, er, in a
Very Real Unreal Sense in this instance, if you are
still with us . . .*

Fortunately, because Jesus was not a late twentieth-
century Protestant clergyman, he never offered any
tosh or drivel remotely like this nonsense to any of
his listeners.

Had he done, the churches would have emptied
like leaking dams . . . before they'd even been
thought of.

14

DISCIPLE: Er, Jesus?

JESUS: Yes, curate. Sorry, jumping ahead of myself;
yes, disciple.

DISCIPLE: I was wondering about the Last Judgement?

JESUS: Yes . . . ?

DISCIPLE: Well, all these people who keep totally
ignoring our message and trying to turn us into a
laughing stock?

JESUS: What's the problem?

DISCIPLE: Well, will it be all right on the night? For
them, like?

VERY REAL SENSES

JESUS: My dear boy, let me put it like this. Our Heavenly Father is like a cleaner getting his house in tip-top shape. At the last judgement, he'll get out his almighty hoover and suck us all up into his love, regardless of what carpet we're hiding under or what we're like.

DISCIPLE: Hang on, Jesus mate, isn't that that old chestnut the theologians will call "Universalism"?

JESUS: Er, sorry?

DISCIPLE: Universalism, you know, the notion that all that heavy stuff about being eternally lost, and punished and judged, is the primitive product of a pre-modern worldview which has no place in the post-mediaeval world. And anyway, what are you doing here if we're all okay come the big J Day? This hoover stuff sounds like God's a bit of a sucker if you ask me.

JESUS: Look, pal, nobody asked you. Now I don't know about anyone else but I could murder a locust-burger.

15

Our Father Richard in Heaven, Harold be thy name . . .
The old ones are the best, eh?

GOD

Ever had a warm fuzzy?
The doctrine of the warm fuzzy took a particular hold
on churchgoers at the tail end of the twentieth
century, with the growth of the so-called charismatic
movement. But it had been known before.

The general idea is that if you are in a religious
meeting with lots of other religious people and you
sing religious songs louder and faster and more and
more often, eventually you'll begin to feel all warm
and fuzzy. Alternatively, if you "go forward" at the
end of a religious meeting to commit your life to
the Maker – the preacher laying his firm hands on
your head, others kneeling around muttering in
strange languages, others gently weeping – you may
also get a warm fuzzy.

This is generally attributed to the presence of the
Holy Spirit. Unfortunately – at least for this
particular theology – warm fuzzies can also be
achieved at football matches when your team goes
into the lead. Or through the use of illegal
substances. Another problem is that many people
who genuinely worship God in cold, damp, empty
church services, or others who commit their lives
to following Jesus and end up in some crappy church
hall dispensing soup to the perpetually ungrateful,

WARM FUZZIES

don't get a warm fuzzy feeling at all.

Which would indicate that the presence of said Spirit and feeling of warm fuzziness may not be one and same.

In fact, the presence of the Spirit is a rather unpredictable business . . . comes along and sweeps you off your feet when you least expect it, and appears to have gone on holiday when you most need to know God is there. Odd really. And often rather more fuzzy than warm.

17

It's better to get drunk in the Holy Spirit but Jack Daniels is sometimes a little easier.

A sentiment with which many would agree, for the simple reason that the Holy Spirit is not available bottled and ready for consumption, even in the 1990s. In fact, try to bottle the Holy Spirit and you're in deep trouble. No doubt some enterprising cleric will give it a go soon. Although Jesus never said this, Bono of U2 did.

18

That's The Spirit.

HOLY SPIRIT

19

I am soon to leave you, but in a little while I will send you The Comforter and he will show you liturgical dance, the acoustic guitar, and help you get to grips with the whole hands-down-for-coffee culture.

20

Anyone fancy a spot of hoovering in the Spirit? This in fact is a late addition to the New Testament understanding of Jesus's ideas, thought to have been inserted into his teachings by resurgent pentecostal churches, who felt there ought to be some biblical justification for the rather unusual humming and buzzing noises emitted from many a house-church meeting when they had moved into overly long times of "prayer and praise".
It appears to have little foundation in the original texts, which may well account for its popularity.

21

If I was in charge of a bookshop, I wouldn't stock this book. No way.

HOLY SPIRIT

22

My Straitjacket I Leave With You.
Jesus could, we suppose, have left his peace with us.
The life-giving peace seen in a beautiful sense of
inner freedom, that results from an openness to God
and a willingness to respond to him.
But, knowing what naughty, bad, wicked people
we are, Jesus thought better of it, and left a
straitjacket instead. Very sensible, very Calvinist,
very Puritan, very fundamentalist. And a smacked
hand for anyone who thinks otherwise.

23

*God moves in mysterious ways. (Particularly on the
dance floor.)*

24

*Have I ever told you about my Big Bang theory, or
my Origin of the Species work . . . well, I'm sure
it'll all be explained by a bright professor called
Steven Hawking in* A Brief History of Time.
'Course it goes without saying that Jesus had a lot
to do with the origin of the species. And the

STRAITJACKETS

continuation of the species and the destination of the species for that matter. But he wasn't particularly big for scientific discussions on the theme.

This may have something to do with the fact that in first century Judaea the influence of modern evolutionary thinking on ideas of where the universe came from and how was not that far advanced. In fact it was quite unadvanced. Behind the times actually. Generally Jesus was not that hot on details – he just assumed things. Like, God created everything somehow and keeps the whole show on the road every day. He told the stories of Adam and Eve but he never disqualified you from the club if you thought they might have been just that – stories.

There were plenty of atheists in those days – just like today – but they had to "come out" then, unlike now when it's the believers who have to "come out". True, they behaved as if God didn't exist, as if Love wasn't watching over us all. Jesus concentrated on reminding them that, as they appeared to have forgotten that Love was above, Love had now come down.

As for writing books about the origins of it all – in thirty-three short years, Jesus Christ *was* A Brief History of Time.

A BRIEF HISTORY OF TIME

25

In the beginning God created the Heavens and the earth and it took seven days, each day consisting of twenty-four hours, each hour consisting of sixty minutes, each minute consisting of sixty seconds. . . .

THE CREATION

26

If you're wondering why arms have hair on them it's not so that it hurts when you pull a plaster off – the real reason is so that kids who don't have a watch can look at their wrist and say (when someone asks them the time) – "It's two freckles past a hair". . . . We thought it was a good idea at the time – and the time was several billion years ago, remember.

27

*It has always baffled me:
(1) how Steven Hawking will manage to hawk so many copies of* A Brief History of Time *without being even remotely right, and moreover
(2) without even issuing it in paperback. . . .
Still, we have got one thing in common. Everyone will have our book, but no one will read it.*

THE CREATION

28

Arthur C. Clarke
Sri Lanka

Dear Arthur C. Clarke,
I saw your excellent 2001 A Space Odyssey. Some-
thing about the film has troubled me for some time
now. How did you manage to get the scene in the
space station with the astronaut running upside down
like that? If you could let me know I'm sure I could
put it to good use in a universe that me and the guys
are working on right now. I won't bore you with the
details.

Best regards,

J. Christ
Inventor

29

Keep Sunday Special.

2001: A SPACE ODYSSEY

30

On the seventh day God got completely, totally, mind–numbingly bored. Hardly surprising, he had nothing to do at all.

This saying of Jesus accounts of course for the fact that down the centuries – and still today for some – there is no playing sports on Sunday, no going to anything entertaining, no buying a newspaper, no going to a shop, no putting the telly on . . . no doing anything that isn't stupendously, humongously, mind-numbingly boring. Sunday means BORING. Surely this is what our Lord meant when he said that "The Sabbath is made for people, not people the Sabbath".

31

The End is nigh . . .

32

And did my feet in ancient times, walk upon England's mountains green?
YES – certainly. Blake was absolutely right. Total anglophile, me. Loved Glastonbury and all that

WILLIAM BLAKE

*West Country mysticism. Druids, ley lines, hairy
people, Stonehenge, folk music festivals, weirdos
generally. Remember – I'm a hippy who never quite
grew up as well!
P.S. I also spent a short time in Palestine. But I've
never been to France. Perish le thought.*

33

The summers were longer then.
The absurd nostalgia of this statement has nothing
to do with Jesus. For behind the words is the
fatuous idea that somehow in the past there was a
goodwill around that just isn't there today. Excuse
the Son of God a derisive smile, please.
After all, two thousand years ago Pilate appealed
to this abundant goodwill of humanity when he said,
"Behold the Man". What happened? The crowd told
him to get stuffed and Jesus to get crucified. Nice.
No, it's a jungle out there. Always has been, always
will be. So never be tempted to trust the world.
Even retrospectively. The idea is to LOVE it – to
love the jungle, just as Jesus did. Even though it
killed him. And in the meantime, to quote something
Jesus did say, be as wise as serpents and as innocent
as doves.

DRUIDS

People aren't so important, you know, there'll be more along in a moment – it's the life-force that counts, isn't it?

Life-forces do have advantages – they don't collect pensions or unemployment benefit and they don't need comforting when they're in distress. But they're no fun to be with either. The life-force has always been a good idea, but not quite as good as the idea that not even a sparrow falls to the ground without God taking notice, that "Every hair is numbered and every grain of sand is counted".

35

Hey, if it feels good do it!

Yes, but what if your feelings aren't all right, like if they're sick, man, know what I mean, like.

I mean, if your feelings are not well, they might tell you that something's right when it's wrong . . . or wrong when it's right. Anyway, faith's not quite as easy as that. What about that stuff about denying yourself, taking up your cross and following him? That stuff about losing your life for his sake in order to find it for your own sake? Hey, if your feelings

THE LIFE FORCE

have got anything to do with it, it doesn't feel good
to do this, man. You dig? I mean, sprouts don't feel
good, but you gotta have greens for a balanced diet.

36

We're just chemicals in the end, just amoebas with the bits mixed up differently.
Yeah? And Science will comfort the lonely and clothe the naked.

37

Us people, we may not be perfect but we can be, if we just have faith in ourselves, in progress, in science. We can become gods ourselves you know, it's only a matter of time . . .
Oh dear, must we? All that responsibility. All those prayers to answer. Wherever would you get the time? Anyway, where's the fun in being God if everyone else is being God too?

38

Holy Mackerel!
Naturally. It's a holy fisherman. Boom. Boom.

AMOEBAS

While we're up in this mountain I'd really like to give you some handy tips my Father and I've jotted down in stone for you to make sure the party down below doesn't get way out of hand – here goes: they're called THE TEN COMMANDMENTS. I don't know why – I named them after a great Hollywood film I knew I was going to see one day. Wasn't Charlton Heston just brilliant?

1 WORSHIP NO GOD BUT ME

You may well have some difficulty with this one. Let me explain: when you go to an Arsenal-Spurs match and there's no score and you're into extra time, and with the final kick of the match by a nameless substitute from in front of the Arsenal goal the wind takes the ball high up over the Spurs midfield and defence, bounces and trickles between the legs of the temporarily-blinded goal-keeper . . . well, what the Arsenal supporters do next is called worship.

If, however, you make the mistake of elevating Arsenal above all else you'll know what the word "God" means. (It might well then be time to ask the question: "Does Arsenal have a plan for your life?" And if you can answer that question you get a free lifetime subscripton to The Church Times.)

THE TEN COMMANDMENTS

2 DO NOT MAKE IMAGES FOR YOURSELF

Instead, adopt the images and values seen in advertising, television and film. These images are obviously more worthy and lasting than anything else – why else would they be so appealing, powerful and prevalent? Ponder for a moment on the wisdom of: "Milky Way. The sweet you can eat between meals without ruining your appetite." Which is obviously so true and helpful to parents trying to encourage their children to have a healthy diet. Or: "Softness is a thing called Comfort." From this we see that the abstract idea of softness is embodied in a blue plastic bottle with a screw cap. Brilliant.

3 DO NOT USE MY NAME FOR EVIL PURPOSES

I'm not really sure where to begin on this one. I feel duty bound to say to begin with that there may be some misunderstanding in some quarters – my middle name does not begin with H, as in "Jesus H. Christ!" So if you're going to use my name, get it right.

4 KEEP SUNDAY SPECIAL

Sunday is the special day for DIY and supermarket shopping. Keep it that way.

KEEP SUNDAY SPECIAL

5 RESPECT YOUR FATHER AND MOTHER

Unless of course your father and mother embarrass you – in which case you have my full permission to treat them with the contempt that they deserve.

6 DO NOT COMMIT MURDER

Murder is terrible. Do not do it. It is almost on a par with theft or financial fraud in the City.

7 DO NOT COMMIT ADULTERY

What we meant to say here was, don't get caught. If however you are a rather wimpish British politician you might find that a bit of old-fashioned adultery does wonders for your campaign and could well tip the balance in an election. I mean, we're all human aren't we, and life does have its pressures.

8 DO NOT STEAL

Again, this really boils down to one of those "don't get caught" things. Though you will find that on an international scale there is no need to get worried about things such as paying ridiculously low prices for goods from people who are too poor or weak to argue about the price of the goods they have made.

ADULTERY

9 DO NOT ACCUSE ANYONE FALSELY

Unless it's essential for your long-term ambitions.

10 DO NOT COVET YOUR NEIGHBOUR'S ASS

You'd look completely stupid with two bums.

11. Oh, and one last one I just want to slip in –
LOVE GOD MORE THAN YOU LOVE GARY LINEKER. OK?

Fairly obvious stuff really, just thought I'd jot it down on stone in case you get stuck for an excuse to condemn somebody or other. No need to get personal about it of course.

40

By their bookshelf will you know them.

41

Call me Reverend – Most Reverend Jesus Christ. PhD (Oxon. R. Lowing).

42

Love is . . . tolerance. We'd all get along a lot better if we were just a bit more tolerant. You mark my words — don't let your convictions get in the way of true dialogue with your fellow humans of differing religious persuasions. If your beliefs are hindering meaningful relational progress, dump them.

43

Greater love hath no man than this, that he give up his seat on the bus for an old lady, or help a blind person across a road or put some money in the charity box at Christmas . . .

Well close, but actually the original version was about laying down your life for your friends. Still, we've all got to start somewhere. . . .

44

No, honestly. Some of my best friends are white. . . .

No. Wrong. None of Jesus's best friends could have been remotely white. It's possible, however, that he has made one or two white friends subsequently.

TOLERANCE

45

Every cloud has a silver lining.
Except those that hover like bad omens above some
people throughout their lives, drenching, soaking
and eventually drowning them.

46

Seeing is believing.
Rot. When did you last see and believe an advert,
for example? And when did you last not believe the
wind in your face? As far as God is concerned, it's
usually more true to say, "Believing is seeing".

47

Always look on the bright side of life.
This was the refrain sung by the thief crucified next
to Brian to cheer him up in the Monty Python film
The Life of Brian. The Monty Python team
strenuously denied that their character Brian was
supposed to be Jesus, to be based vaguely on Jesus,
er, in fact, to have anything whatsoever to do with
Jesus. Jesus who? Looked a bit suspicious though.
Perhaps the Pythons would be interested to know

THE LIFE OF BRIAN

the song he actually sang at the time, which was
much more catchy. Something about, "Father,
forgive them, they don't know what they're
doing. . .".

48

*Let those of you with ears to hear block them up
with something. But do plan on doing something
about what I say, tomorrow maybe, or perhaps next
week. Or next year. When things are less busy. . .*

49

Fools rush in where angels fear to tread.
Sorry? Now where would an angel fear to tread? Eh?

50

Cleanliness is next to Godliness.
Actually, it's usually next to the soap.

51

Blessed Are The Tee-Totallers For They Won't Be Caught Drink-Driving. (Although, between you and me, I don't mind a nice glass of red at a wedding myself.)

51

Read my lips. No new taxes.
And you could trust Jesus on this one – he hung out with a lot of tax-collectors.

52

Blessed are the Non-Smokers, for the Body is a Temple of the Holy Spirit, and how would you like it if your house was full of smoke all the time?

53

I'm very fond of my pigs, but I don't find it difficult to eat them.
When the former Archbishop of Canterbury, Lord Runcie, said this, there is no compelling evidence

to suggest he was quoting Jesus. Indeed, there is some pretty strong evidence to the contrary. (See food laws in the Old Testament.)

Sausage rolls weren't in fact on the Christian menu, until Paul got hold of it. Once he did, and Peter joined in as well, culinary options were extended considerably. More pig, vicar?

54

Blessed are those of you who don't go to the cinema (unless it's Chariots of Fire) *because you are Puritans. You can't be too careful out there.*

55

Blessed are the vegetarians, although I like a nice piece of mutton at Passover myself.

56

Be as good as you can.
Well, sounds plausible doesn't it? Maybe that's why he never said it.

VEGETARIANS

57

Let me tell you about The Kingdom of Cod.
Actually this is another mishearing of Jesus – like
"Blessed are the Cheesemakers" – which is again
perfectly understandable in a community of fishing
people, especially when Jesus often invited them to
become fishers of men. About as meaningful as going
to the chippie and asking for "Two portions of God
and chips please".

58

Seek Suffering.
Actually, no. Seek God. There *is* a difference.

59

*Blessed are those of you who grow a beard to model
yourselves on me.*
Especially if you're a woman.

60

As my followers you really ought to wear sensible clothing.

Remember, be practical – sensible shoes, tweed skirt, plain colours, no buttons. And similar if you're a woman. Keep a fig-leaf handy in case of emergency.

61

When your hair looks good, you feel good.

Thought now by historians *not* to date back to John the Baptist (who had genuine problem-hair through long-term lack of attention), but rather to a shampoo advert in the 1970s. It is therefore unlikely to have been familiar to our Lord during his earthly ministry, despite his extraordinary powers in seeing events ahead of time.

Not that he would have used it anyway. It is not only tosh. It is BALDIST tosh . . . (or is that HAIRIST?)

62

Why is it that Americans think they have a special deal with me and my dad and deserve favourable

*judgement terms? I'm looking at the account right
now and it still seems to be rather overdrawn.*

63

*If you're going to San Francisco,
Be sure to wear a flower in your hair.*
These opening lines from the famous song are about
as deep as the 1960s managed to get with regard to
the meaning of life. Less convincing now of course,
but follow their advice and at least you'll give the
current residents of San Francisco a good laugh.
Whether the original St Francis, and his guide
Jesus, will also be laughing is, er, less certain. There's
a thin line between the foolish and the fatal.

64

*Now, about manners – always be polite, be
courteous, be nice.*
Well, this may be the kind of role-model your vicar
has adopted but there's little biblical precedent for
it. The powerful "Gentle Jesus, meek and mild"
School of Theology is largely discredited these days,
as our Lord is more often portrayed as a radical
political liberator of the oppressed, in the latest Che

FLOWER POWER

Guevara look. (Very late in his case.) Regardless of the twists and turns in the way he is portrayed by his followers, in fact the biblical record suggests that at times Jesus was rude, sarcastic, abrasive, awkward and a bit of a know-all. (No prizes for guessing the reasons for the last one!) Mind you, he was also kind, attentive, peace-loving, patient and long-suffering. Altogether a pretty mixed-up kinda guy. Still, a lot more colourful than our usual images of him.

65

Always look for the best in someone, never criticize them – what good can come of it?
Er, quite a bit in the case of whitened sepulchres for example.

66

It's a sex-mad world out there, all right – keep those ankles covered.

CHE GUEVARA

67

Sex is different, everybody – all right?
Sex is different.
Sex, I'm afraid, is one of those areas – perhaps the only one in fact – where things are very cut and dried. Sorry about that folks – but, er, rules is rules, as they say.
Personally, I'm not a great one for rules, you know that. Generally, it's attitudes that I'm interested in. But – call me old-fashioned – I've got this real thing about sex. That's why I'm always condemning everyone concerning it. Maybe I just haven't worked it through myself. I don't know.
Anyway, that's your problem, lads and lasses, because from here on, it's straitjacket and rules time. And if that means the whole business goes hush-hush, tut-tut, naughty-naughty and under the rug, then so be it.
Bit awkward, I'm afraid, but as I say, sex is definitely different.

68

Always Use a Condom.

SEX IS DIFFERENT

69

Sex, I think you'll find, is really rather dirty and to be avoided if at all possible, except in the cause of the continuation of the species. And then only with your eyes shut and without for a second enjoying it.

70

Every sperm is sacred.

71

If you find yourself of a non-heterosexual inclination, you'd better switch across to the heterosexual inclination as soon as possible. Far less hassle all around.

72

AIDS, well, I don't think it takes too much thinking about to realize that it's almost certainly judgement from on high for unacceptable sexual habits.
Well, what else could it be? And acne is judgement for looking in the mirror too much. And blindness

is judgement for. . . . (Thank you, that's quite
enough, *Ed.*)

73

Sex will sell almost everything, I think you'll find.
Ooops! This one slipped in from The Gospel
According to Advertising.

74

*You really should keep your private bits covered up
at all times, you know – otherwise they won't be
private, will they?*

75

Did Martin Scorcese get it right in The Last
Temptation of Christ? *Did I really marry and settle
down as a family man after all? I'm afraid I can't
tell you if he got it right or not – because people
made such a fuss about the movie being blasphemous
that it never got to my local cinema. However, I
liked* Raging Bull *and* Taxi Driver *very much. Nice
work, Marty. Is De Niro really as odd in private as
people say he is?*

THE LAST TEMPTATION OF CHRIST

76

*The meek will inherit the earth, if that's all right
with the rest of you.*
Fortunately for the meek, he stopped talking after
the first clause.

77

If there's one thing I can't stand it's adultery. . . .
Well, there were quite a few things Jesus couldn't
stand actually – hypocrisy was high up on the list,
higher still was religious hypocrisy, then there were
corrupt financial practices, empty, hollow piety,
turning his Father's house into a market place, rich

ADULTERY

people who ignored the poor on their doorstep, television evangelists (er, it's in there somewhere . . .), personal violence, jostling for rank and position, saying you'll do something and then not doing it, lying, starting wars . . . we could go on. 'Course, he wasn't exactly wild about adultery either, but when he came across someone about to be stoned for it, he stared down her accusers and suggested to her that, sin though it was, popping out her brains with pebbles probably wouldn't help her future sexual identity that much.

78

Anyone divorced might as well forget any idea of divine love.
Or of becoming a priest in the Church of England for that matter. Or monarch, Head of the Church of England. Funny that, because you can go to gaol for fraud or even murder, serve your time, get called to the cloth and, if the powers that be think it's the real McCoy, you're in. No further questions asked, my friend. (As it should be, too, otherwise what's the point of having a faith with forgiveness bang in the middle of it?) Unless, that is, you're a convicted murderer who's also divorced. . . .

TELEVISION EVANGELISTS

79

Be a hooker for me.
Actually one of the rather numerous heresies of the Children of God cult. But it certainly did wonders for recruitment.

80

Keep women in the kitchen, certainly not in the pulpit.
One of the numerous heresies of the mainstream churches. Done nothing for recruitment.

81

Go to church. You'll find walking along on a Sunday morning to sit in rows for an hour and twenty minutes in a freezing cold building is an extremely important way of coming to understand the meaning of life. The daft words that you will be asked to sing in these songs with a heavy Radio 2 influence will be of enormous value in understanding more fully the eternal mysteries, particularly suffering and the question, "Why is the music so naff?" I'm thinking of such classics as

CHURCH

Be cold, be cold,
be strong, be strong
For the Lord thy God is with you . . . .

— these kind of songs are brilliant at communicating truth; they really get to the heart of belief. It is through keeping the heating turned right down, or preferably off, that we are forced to find an inner strength to endure the hardship. It may be of interest to know that though you may be freezing in your seat the clergy(man) probably isn't. For a start he/she will be on their feet and moving about which keeps them warmer, and they will quite often be wearing a form of dress that has not been seen in normal life for a few hundred years. Contrary to what you might have heard, vestments are not worn for any symbolic reason but just because (as any skier will know) lots of thin layers of clothing are much warmer than one thick sweater or coat. Anyway, Vicarages and Manses are always freezing.

82

Looking around me now as I sit on this Galilean hillside, I see a disappointing lack of hard and immovable long chair-like things. More generally I see around me a land crying short of cold, bleak

CHURCH

stone buildings used – with difficulty – once a week.
Still, be of good cheer, my friends, and have faith.
Surely the good news I bear must one day bring
forth both of these. Let the former be called "Pews"
and the latter "Churches". Let there be much
discomfort caused by the first, and much frustration
by the outdatedness of the second. Oh, and let there
be much rejoicing too. If it's at all possible.

83

You Must Be Bored Again.
Another mishearing this one. What he actually said
was, "You must be born again . . .", a phrase that
has been thoroughly devalued and stripped of all
meaning by the bizarre antics of many born-
againites at the end of the twentieth century. And
it's not so difficult to understand why people
mishear this one – despite the dramatic change that
is supposed to have occurred in them at "re-birth",
many of them soon look distinctly like everyone else
in church, bored again and again, week after week.

BEING BORED AGAIN

84

My own feeling, Peter, is that those in power should be trusted. No, really. Undue cynicism can be very damaging. So if anyone ever suggests that I called Herod a "fox" or referred to the worthy religious leaders of my day as, amongst other things, "imposters, blind guides and white washed tombs full of dead men's bones" – er, don't believe them. I mean, I'm sorry but that's just being negative, isn't it? Too easy. Much too easy. Nothing creative or helpful in that at all, quite frankly. If you can't say something nice, don't say it at all – that's my motto.

85

JESUS: *I did not tell you a lot of things at the beginning, because I was with you. Now, however, I must leave you. Leaving is sad. But I tell you the truth – it is better for you that I go away. Because if I do not go, the Helper will not come to you. But if I do go away, then the Helper will come. I will send him. He is the third member of the Trinity.*

DISCIPLES: You will send to us the third member of the Trinity?

BLIND GUIDES

JESUS: *Indeed.*

DISCIPLES: You mean, you will send us your – your Spirit?

JESUS: *You must be joking. Couldn't trust you with that, you beggars. No, no, no – I'll send the Bible. Father, Son – and Bible.*

86

My Church is the repository of all truth.
This text has been badly translated from the Aramaic. What Jesus actually said was "My Church is the suppository of all truth", meaning of course that the Church's rightful place in society is not to the front, not in the limelight at all. This "suppository gospel" – as it is sometimes called – suggests that Jesus wanted his Church to avoid being publicly showy, rather to work quietly in hidden places – backing up the truth, as it were, getting to the bottom of things without people knowing, necessarily, that anything is happening at all. The image of the suppository quietly melting in a smelly place to benefit the truth is a powerful one. Jesus's hearers at the time would have enjoyed his rude joke at the expense of the Church.

THE BIBLE

Sometimes, lads, people say to me, "Where can I find God?" A fine question, that, "Where can I find God?" And the short answer, of course, is this: in the countryside. That's where you find God. The sunsets can be very pretty in the countryside and there aren't any people to spoil the view or to make demands. God loves pretty things. God loves undemanding things, so in the countryside is generally where you'd find him. Or at least in areas where the schools have smart uniforms, proper assemblies, and good exam results. God loves to hang around those sorts of places as well. I mean, basically, God loves all things "nice", if you know what I mean – and I think you do.

So, as I say, if you want to find God – and I'm delighted that you do, absolutely thrilled in fact, because it's a beautiful, beautiful desire – think sunsets, think undemanding, think good schools, think "nice". And don't, whatever you do, look for God under your own nose. Or in anything which is remotely painful.

GOD

JESUS: *So, Christmas is coming, Archie. Just how does a great artist like yourself grasp the essence of Christmas on canvas?*

ARCHIE: The essence of Christmas? You mean the holy stable and the celebration of the angels? You mean, the skies alight with praise at this in-break of God into the world – the shepherds agog with awe and the wise men struck with amazement? In short, the sheer wonder and mystery of God becoming human?

JESUS: *Indeed. How do you, as a man of the world, capture such depths and such heights on a simple canvas?*

ARCHIE: Well, usually I paint a robin alongside a whopping great mince pie.

JESUS: *That's brilliant.*

89

*For myself, I prefer the word "victim" to "sinner".
I don't believe in calling people "sinners". Has such
unhelpful connotations. Nasty, nasty word. It kind
of suggests that someone needs to change and I
can't buy that one at all, I'm afraid. No, "sinner" is*

CHRISTMAS

a real cold shower of a word, a real "party pooper".
Whereas "victim" – now that can be everyone's
friend. Much more cosy. Much more
accommodating. Everything is someone else's fault,
you see. So take yourself for instance. You're fine,
You're absolutely fine. It's them. And them. And
them. They're the ones who ought to get their act
together. And pretty damn quick too. Whereas you
– you can just lie back and feel sorry for yourself.
Designating yourself a "victim" – well, it's almost as
good as a piping hot bath, isn't it?

So, yes, I much prefer the word "victim" to
"sinner". In fact, it's totally brilliant being a victim,
once you get the hang of it. Victims never have to
say sorry. Victims can just whine, demand, have
tantrums, and generally fritter away their energy in
the noble pursuit of themselves and in all things
pertaining thereunto.

So next time you feel a pang of conscience about
something, don't say "sinner". Don't even entertain
the thought that you might be partially responsible
for the direction of your life. No, no and thrice no.
No – simply cry "victim". Simpy cry loud and clear,
"I'm a victim, all right?" And discover therein the
passport to paradise.

Jesus did say: "If you do not turn from your sins,
you will all die."

SINS

SSSSSSSHHHHH! This is a place of worship!
It's a little-known fact that Jesus spent most of his
time hanging around the backs of cathedrals and
churches. He did this for a particular purpose – so
he could stick his finger in front of his mouth and
say, "Sshhh!" in an irritated voice to anyone
displaying the least signs of human life. After all,
how could ANYONE worship (i.e. "give worth") to
God through jollity and laughter? Precisely. Case
closed. That's why Jesus NEVER went to wedding
receptions, of course. Never, ever, EVER. So sshh!
everyone. SSSHHH! . . .

91

*About church, just to be on the safe side, you're best
off going twice a week . . . oh, and once mid-week
just to be absolutely sure. . . .*
Who knows where this strange tradition began, but
by the middle of the twentieth century it was so
firmly established in many Christian traditions that
a lie-in on a Sunday morning had become
tantamount to mass-murder or, worse still, not
reading your Bible every day.

WORSHIP

In one sense Jesus never actually went to church at all. He didn't have to. He is Church, if you see what we mean. He did go along to the synagogue, of course, not to keep up appearances but to alert the other synagogue-goers as to the strange times they were in and his unique role in it. On one occasion, before he had even reached his teens, he started another long-standing tradition in getting ticked off by his parents for his attitude to the morning service at the Temple. Oddly, it was for hanging around too long! In fact he did tell one of his followers, Peter, that he was the kind of solid character – Peter! – on which he could really get something like a movement going, what later got called Church. But despite the work of thousands of theologians and archaeologists, despite the revelations in the Dead Sea Scrolls and other ancient documents, no one has yet come up with any hint that Jesus told his followers to be there at 11 o'clock on Sunday morning or face the wrath of the Almighty.

92

Let there always be coffee after church – and let it always be too weak.

COFFEE THEOLOGY

93

St Peter has a great deal to answer for. When I asked him to establish the Jesus Fan Club I sort of hoped he'd take a different approach to the one he did. Still, when you work with amateurs what can you expect? The one good thing I can say is I like the logo. The music used to be good about 600 years ago, but since then things seem to have got stuck in a rut somewhat. The clothes also are a blast from the past rather than the blast from the future that they could have been.

94

FRANK: Jesus Christ.

JESUS: *Yes, my son.*

FRANK: May I ask you a question?

JESUS: *Be frank, Frank.*

FRANK: I'll be frank if you'll be frank.

JESUS: *You're very earnest, Frank.*

FRANK: Will you be frank, Jesus?

JESUS: *Frank as I can be, Frank.*

FRANK: OK, here goes: Jesus what is life all about?

JESUS: *I'm glad you asked that, Frank. You put your left foot in. . . .*

ST PETER

FRANK: Your left foot in. . . .

JESUS: *You put your left foot out.*

FRANK: You put your left foot out. . . .

JESUS: *In, out, shake it all about.* . . .

FRANK: In, out, shake it all about. . . .

JESUS: *You do the hokey kokey.* . . .

FRANK: . . . Wait, wait . . . and . . . and . . . And turn yourself around!

JESUS: *Yes, you're getting it, you're getting it!*

TOGETHER: *That's what it's all about!*

The camera pulls back to reveal them standing in front of an old Victorian church. They turn and walk in at the door, skipping and gambolling. Crowds of people are walking in, some have three heads, or nine legs, others are clearly aliens from outer space.

We see these words supered on the scene: "Your local church. Strange but true."

HOKEY KOKEY THEOLOGY

95

I wanna tell you a sermon. . . .
Which is what most clergymen want to do for the benefit of their congregation, but unfortunately their congregation, going on past experience, rarely want the benefit. That's because their stories don't have a beginning, middle and end, or, er, any likeable characters or, er, interesting places, or any movement or drama or anything storylike at all really. . . . They're just talks telling you what to believe and where to sign on the dotted line.

Jesus, in contrast, told tons of strange stories, so strange that half of the time no one had a clue what he was on about. They were about virgins and foreigners, about people burning in hell, or dying and abandoned on the roadside, about millionaires and about people on the unleavened breadline. . . . And if you didn't understand, well he didn't bother explaining. He'd mutter infuriating explanations when pressed, like "He who has ears to hear. . . ." Fine, thanks a bunch. But they were a talking point. Maybe that's why people remembered them and why people still discuss them.

Unlike most sermons.

SERMONS

96

*OK, OK – I'm twenty minutes into my parable now,
so we'll have a silly kiddies' song, and then could
the Sunday School leave for their own activities?
Because from here on, the words I use in the
parable are going to be rather long, abstract and
largely incomprehensible.*

97

Our Father in Heaven,

*May your name be really, Lord, just – well – be
hallowed today,
And really Lord, may your Kingdom just come,
And may your will just be done, in a most remarkable
and decisive way, Lord,
On earth, as really, Lord, it is in Heaven, Lord.
And we just pray that you really will give us today
our daily bread,
And may you really just forgive us our sins, Lord,
As we just really, Lord, forgive the sins of others,
And may you really, Lord, just not lead us into
temptation in a most remarkable, decisive way,
Lord,
But deliver us from evil,*

SUNDAY SCHOOL

For really, Lord, we just lay claim to that eternal and abiding truth written across the very soul of scripture that yours really is the Kingdom and it really is just the power and the great, er, glory, in a most completely remarkable and decisive way, Lord.
Now and just really for ever.
A-just-really-Lord-men.

98

Honk If You Love Me.

99

I'm teetotal myself.
On one occasion, at a wedding of some old friends, Jesus instantly brewed gallons of his own wine (Chateau Cana AD 31 – a vintage year) which was said to be better than the cheap plonk they'd been drinking earlier. And it was cheaper than Sainsbury's. Good wine costs less in the New Testament.

TEETOTALISM

Let's not beat about the burning bush, people, there's money in this religion business – and once you've got followers following, you ought to be thinking about equity, cash-flow, capital assets and land, lots of land, with lots of buildings on it, with spires and crosses and weather vanes atop . . . that's my advice anyway.

And if you believe that, you'll believe anything.

How is it that an organization which claims to follow in the footsteps of someone who made no bones about the fact that he had nowhere to lay his head, has, in the West at least, become one of the wealthiest in the world?

How come Bishops live in palaces and sit on thrones and wear flashy gear?

How come they have to bother themselves with cash-flow and stock-market portfolios when their · members can barely be bothered to reach into their pockets for some loose change for the collection plate?

How come they sound so plausible when they preach sermons about what Jesus meant, *really* meant, when he said, "It is easier for a camel to pass through the eye of a needle than for a rich person to enter the Kingdom of God"?

RELIGION AND MONEY

How come we can sit here writing this stuff
pointing fingers when all the fingers are pointing
back at us?

101

*Earn as much as you can, get a big house and a nice
car with a customized number-plate. Go on, you're
talented, you deserve it.*
No, you've got the wrong end of the stick with this
one. What he actually said was, "Sell all you have
and give it to the poor and come follow me".

102

Jesus saves.
That's true. But who with? You can't trust any of the
banks these days.

103

*So once the Levite and the priest had passed by on
the other side of the road from the injured man, a
Samaritan turned up. He was The Good Samaritan,
in fact, and so as soon as he saw the injured man,
he knelt down beside him and gently said, "The
wages of sin is death."*

THE BANK OF JESUS

104

These days everything is so expensive I'm often asked is it worth putting small amounts of money into the collection. Well, the answer is no. Anything under about £50 is hardly worth the administration. It is even better if it is covenanted.

105

If someone brings a lawsuit against you – take out a counter-suit against them – and don't let the beggars get you down.

106

It's all down to market forces. . . .
Another easily-made mistake in the old mental cross-referencing here. Jesus was particularly concerned about force in the market – he used it to overturn the tables of the traders in the Temple for turning it into such – but it was Mrs Thatcher, that great spiritual leader of the 1980s, who believed in the doctrine of market forces. This led her to one of her most profound theological insights, that the reason the Good Samaritan could be good was because he

MARKET FORCES

had the money (no doubt a big noise in the City)
to help the poor man on the road.

Mrs T's "trickle-down" theory of economics held
that as she helped the rich get richer, so their
wealth would eventually (she never said how long it
might take – one or two millennia perhaps?) trickle
down, through their extraordinary beneficence, to
the, er, lower orders of society.

In contrast Jesus had a "splash-it-all-over"
economic theory which talked of the poor being
blessed, and described banquets where the snotty
rich couldn't be bothered to turn up but the hobos
and down-and-outs turned up in droves and got the
best seats. Apparently this is because, unlike Mrs
Thatcher, God's economic theory has this big thing
called Mercy in it. It isn't all about just deserts. Or
just puddings for that matter.

107

Money is the Root of all Evil.
Funny that. Because you'd think Jesus should have
said it. Someone important should've, anyway. After
all, money often seems to be in the undergrowth of
all evil, if not actually at the roots of it. But Jesus
never said much about it. There was some stuff about

paying Caesar his dues, some stuff about the
widow's mite, about Zacchaeus the corrupt tax-
collector paying restitution. . . .

Jesus was a mile away from being Managing
Director of Disciples Inc. with one eye permanently
on the collection-flow. He would have failed any
business exams. He was a useless economist – by
today's standards.

The most money that ever came near Jesus was
the thirty pieces of silver paid for information on
his exact location on that dreadful night near the end
– and Jesus never got to see that. All the disciples
had a common purse but – talk about holy fools –
Judas was in charge of it. Wholly bonkers, more
like. But, like Jesus, they tried to live simply – bit
of fishing here and there – and were grateful for
any food or funds any supporters might pass on. They
never scorned money as if it was evil. They just
never chased after it as if it was good.

108

*We should imitate our Father in Heaven, who, I
might tell you, is absolutely loaded – get my drift?*

DOSH

109

The devil dances in an empty pocket.
This old proverb suggests that poverty leads to temptation and crime and therefore has the devil leaping in delight. Jesus's version, though, would have had Satan dancing even more ecstatically in a full pocket. For it is greed, rather than poverty, that really gets the Destroyer doing the hippy-hippy shake.

110

The poor, well, they'll always be with us, it's the only life they know, they're better off like that. I mean, what's the advantage in being wealthy if everyone is wealthy. Stands to reason, dunnit?

111

Friends, I wanna tell you – if you've got enough faith, these can be yours – wealth, health, a customized number-plate . . . they're a 100 per cent, cast-iron, rootin-tootin, hand-clapping, foot-stompin, God-given certainty.
Strange as it may seem, this kind of thinking is quite

WONGA

popular in some sections of the Church these days. Who knows what Bible they're reading? Who cares?

It's a pretty insulting thing to believe, if you think about it. For a start it suggests that most Christians in the world haven't got any faith. After all, Christians in Africa, for example, are just as ravaged by starvation and famine as everybody else on that continent. However great their faith, it doesn't transport them magically to a Chinese restaurant in London's West End when mealtimes roll around. Anyway, faith in God isn't like Uri Geller bending spoons. You can't sit there urging your faith to increase. Faith comes from your experience of being friends with God. You can't be great friends with someone instantly, on demand. It takes time. Anyway, who wants a customized number-plate?

<u>112</u>

Don't worry 'bout a thing,
'Cos every little thing's
Gonna be all right . . .

Bob Marley, in fact. But not so far off the mark. As our Lord did say,
"Don't worry about tomorrow, each day has enough trouble of its own."

LOOT

113

I wonder if I've ever let you into my Galilean fish-mouth-denarii economic theory?
Think about it.

114

Render unto Caesar that which is Caesar's – unless you can spot any loopholes – and treat yourself with the rest, and drop a few bob in the charity box now and again. . . .

115

I'm only human . . .
Hmmm. Well, this one really opens up a can of theological worms. Because Jesus was of course only human. Er, but he was also . . . not. Not only human but divine, that is. At least that's what his followers have said down the centuries and that's what most of them say today. No point getting into all the rows they've had in the Church about how the human and divine were exactly mixed up in the unique ingredients of Jesus's life, but suffice it to say that Jesus never had to say he was only human because

MAZOOMA

nobody doubted he was human . . . but they still had the strongest suspicions he wasn't *only* human.

116

About Jesus Boots. How come I've never made a penny from this popular piece of merchandizing that has long traded on my name? Time for a word with Ralph Lauren or Coco Chanel.

117

Do as I say, not as I do.
Might sound plausible coming from anyone else perhaps, useful let-out from hypocrisy and all that, but in fact Jesus was the one Person who didn't have any skeletons in his cupboard, no dark sinful secrets he daren't risk anyone finding out. He wasn't the kind of vicar who tells you we're all gifted but then won't let anyone else do anything in the service, and then shouts his head off at his wife after the service, or the youth group leader who tells you not to be tempted into going too far with your boyfriend, and then you find he's got his own girlfriend in the club.

No, Jesus didn't have any credibility problems, there was no faint whiff of hypocrisy on this boy. If he said "Love your enemies" you could bet your bottom denarii he was doing his best to love his. If he said "Do your good deeds in private without boasting about them" you could be pretty confident he wasn't giving a press conference to the *Jerusalem Times* about his latest charitable donations.

So he didn't need qualifying suggestions and caveats like telling people to do as he said, not as he did. He practised what he preached, so he boldly told people shocking stuff like "Imitate me as I imitate God".

You couldn't knock his confidence, could you?

118

My father was a carpenter, I am a carpenter. . . . If you want to follow me, you should all take up carpentry.

119

M: So you're thirty, Jesus – and you say you're going public?

J: *Correct, Mick.*

M: But how? I mean, how are you going to make an impression on history?

CARPENTRY

J: *Well, what have others done?*
M: Others? Well, they've tended to lead huge armies, build massive monuments to themselves or write books.
J: *Correct again Mick. Clever boy.*
M: You mean?
J: *Precisely.*

120

John the Baptist? I bet he drinks Carling Black Label.
Despite his reputation for being the original Iron Man, scholars generally believe that John kept off the non-non-alcohol stuff (his Nazirite Vow banned it actually) and had a penchant for his own special "locust and honey on the rocks".

121

I'm just doing my bit for mankind.
Talk about understatement. Bit like saying electricity's useful if you want to turn the light on, or there's quite a number of people in China.

CARLING BLACK LABEL

122

Can I try some hyperbole out on you?
Okay, try me. "It is easier for a camel to pass through the eye of a needle than for a rich man to enter the kingdom of heaven." Nifty. It's also given the hump (geddit?) to lots of rich people.

123

Jesus is on the cross. Thieves on both
sides. The sky is turning purple as
the sun sinks. A crowd has
gathered. Centurions with beautiful
blood-red plumes stand manfully at
the bottom of the crosses showing
off their beautiful breastplates.

Cut to Jesus. Looks into the camera.
An orchestra strikes up. Jesus sings.

And now, the end is here,
and as I face the final curtain,
my friend, I'll say it clear,
I'll state my case of which I'm certain:
I've lived a life that's full,
I've travelled each and every highway,

HYPERBOLE

And more, much more than this,
I did it my way.

I've loved, I've laughed and cried,
I've had my fill, my share of losing,
and now as tears subside
I find it all so amusing
to think I did all this,
and may I say, not in a shy way,
Oh no, Oh no, not me,
I did it my way.

Yes there were times,
I'm sure you knew,
when I bit off
more than I could chew,
But through it all when there was doubt
I ate it up and spat it out.
The record shows
I took the blows
and did it my way

Regrets, I've had a few,
but then again, too few to mention.
I did what I had to do
and saw it through
without exemption.
I faced each final task,

HIS WAY

each careful step
along the byway,
and more, much more than this,
I did it my way.

For what is a man?
What has he got
if not himself?
Then he has not.
To share the things he truly feels
and not the words of one who kneels.
And through it all
I stood tall
and did it my way.

The Right Reverend and Most Holy Frank Sinatra:
Theologian of the Year.

124

I'm afraid I fail to see the joke.
No, Jesus always saw the joke. He told them, enjoyed
them and saw them. (Remember the one about the
fat man, the needle and the camel? Er, yes, we've
only just had it.) And of course, by his getting up
again after the Cross – the ultimate banana skin –
he's enabled us to laugh at jokes all the more
heartily ever since.

BANANA SKINS

125

On the Cross: *"Happiness is a cigar called Hamlet."*
He DID say – "My God, my God – why have you
abandoned me?" But that's really not as catchy,
is it?

126

"Don't follow me – I'm lost too!!!"
Popular Judaean car-sticker in the first century, still
pretty common today too. But it wasn't on Jesus's
bumper.

127

*Me? I'm everyone's mate, I am. Everyone's favourite
mucker. A bit of this, a bit of that, you know the sort
of thing. Into everything, I am. I've got more fingers
in more pies than the pastry chef at the Bethlehem
Hilton. Jiggery-pokery with bread and fishes – well,
it keeps the punters happy. All done with mirrors,
that one, as it goes. Clever, eh? And of course I tell
a story. Everyone loves a story. Simple folk. Putty
in my hands. Oh, and a bit of healing never goes
amiss, does it? Especially the kiddies. Everyone
loves a kiddies' healing. They're all over me after one*

HAMLET

88

of those. Keeps me in beer for weeks. That's not done by mirrors, that stunt. No – it's done with this strong herbal powder. I put it on the end of my fingers, then stick it up their nose. That soon releases a few "devils". It pays to lay on the EVIL bit nice and thick beforehand – makes for more of a show. Well, it keeps the people happy and earns me a few bob along the way. After all, everyone's got to live.

And if the ladies are rather partial to the old "spiritual guru" figure, then I for one ain't arguing. I'll tell you something, which you may or may not believe. Most nights, I have a choice.

So, I'll tell a fortune here, bull on about a star sign there – they go radio rental for all that stuff. In, out, in, out, shake it all about, that's what I say. If they want crystals, they'll have crystals. If they want reincarnation – don't laugh – they'll have reincarnation. If they want higher spiritual plains, no problem. I use a basic pot pourri mixture for that – hate the pong myself but there are some as likes it. The weird and the wonderful is my stock in trade – anything, in fact, so long as it pays. So what's your fancy then?

Jesus did say, though, that he came not to be served but to serve. And, if it's possible to hold the two comments together, that he is the Way, the Truth and the Life. . . .

THE WAY, THE TRUTH AND THE LIFE

If I ruled the world,
Every day would be the first day of Spring. . . .
Er, no, that was someone altogether different. Mind
you, Jesus was offered the world at one point. But
he declined the offer. Seemed to think there was a
catch in it.

129

There was a moment in the Sixties (the nineteen-
sixties) when I seriously thought my popularity was
threatened by The Beatles. Nasty moment that. You
have to watch these popularity polls, you know.

130

My God, my God why have you forsaken me? This
is just an awful, awful mistake. It wasn't so bad
when I was being followed round by crowds but I
really regret the way things have turned out . . .
now I realize that I am just an ordinary man – a
very good but nevertheless ordinary human being.
How could I have imagined I was your Son?

THE BEATLES

131

I am the Lord of the Dance (said he).
No, he didn't.

132

*Water into wine! The famous "Bread and Fish"
routine! Roll up! Roll up!*
Actually, Jesus was a bit touchy about the odd
miracle he used to do. He worried that word would
get round that he was a bit of a thrill to watch
perform, and that he'd start getting the Paul Daniels
audience in, or even, heaven forbid, Doris Stokes'
fans. He wasn't that keen at all on being thought of
as some kind of wonder-worker, a sort of Superman
in sandals and robes. Very nervous indeed about
getting an image as someone who did wonder-
working. In fact he was so touchy that he even used
to tell people to shut up about what he'd done for
them. Hardly a good tactic for getting news out –
a decent press conference could have done wonders
for his ministry.

LORD OF THE DANCE

I can't go out like this, I need some more blue in my eyes – where's that make-up girl gone?

A lot of people perceive Jesus as the wide-screen, Zeffirelli-ized, Robert Powellized, blow-dried, made-up, neat and handsome, movie-idolized Hollywood version, wind in his golden locks and blue contacts in his eyes. In fact we don't know very much at all about his appearance – odd really when so many people claim to have met him. How did they know it was him?

Jesus probably looked pretty much like any other first-century labouring man, maybe a bit more bleary-eyed from all the late-night prayer-sessions and desert-stomping, but otherwise a regular first-century Jew. John the Baptist was probably a bit of a tailor's nightmare by all accounts, with lumpy honey and dead locusts tangled in his beard from last week's lunch, and a VWM – Visible Water Mark – on his outfit from all the baptisms. But Jesus wasn't notable for his appearance – neither hobo nor Hollywood halo. It was something else that made Jesus seem special.

ROBERT POWELL

134

"Jesus Christ, Superstar, who are you, what are you fighting for. . . ?"
Actually these words were put in the mouths of our Lord's followers by Tim Rice and Andrew Lloyd Webber. It's not clear what their source material was. But who cares? It made them an awful lot of money.

135

Never has anybody spoken like this man.
Like everything else in this book, Jesus didn't say that. But those who heard him did.

136

If I begin to go bald, I think I'll comb my hair forward. I really respect people who do that.

137

JESUS: *I'm soon to die, Archie.*
ARCHIE: Soon to die?
JESUS: *I think so, yes.*

JESUS CHRIST SUPERSTAR

ARCHIE: I'm moved, Master. Greatly moved.

JESUS: *And how will you respond, Archie?*

ARCHIE: As a great artist, you mean?

JESUS: *Yes, as an artist and as a man of the world.*

ARCHIE: How will I respond to the ugly killing of the one who came as a servant to the world, but found love repaid by spite; found challenge repaid by deaf ears and closed minds; found the offer of freedom repaid by the frenzied recourse to legal execution?

JESUS: *Yes. How will you portray all that on canvas?*

ARCHIE: Well, the obvious angle, I suppose, is a few flowers, an Easter bunny and a ruddy great chocolate egg.

JESUS: *That's brilliant.*

138

Of course you know, I'm older than I look . . . people often comment.

Odd as it may seem, there's something in this. After all, if he was the Word of God coming down from the Father, like it says in the Gospel of John, then he was the Word in the beginning – which was quite a long time ago, long before Mary's visit from the wise men. Pretty cosmic eh?

EASTER BUNNIES

139

I hope to live to a ripe old age.

140

Wanna see a trick with leprosy? Now you see it, now you don't.

141

Now here's one with a blind man. Now you don't see, now you do! Boom boom!

142

Watch your step. You wouldn't want to crush a beetle.

143

Winner takes all.
No. Loser takes all. Winners have had their slice of cake already. So pick up that cross today – and start losing. . . .

WINNER TAKES ALL

144

I thank God I'm British.
Jesus was a Jew who lived in occupied Palestine at
a time when Britain was a rather badly organized
bog. Robert Powell (no relation) is British and an
actor. Neither Jesus nor Robert said the above,
however. It was Prince Charles. (P'raps now he'll
write a Foreword? *Ed.*)

145

*Come the Revolution, you'll be first up against the
wall. . . .*
Well, yes, another easy mistake. Jesus did talk about
a revolution, he was all for it – revolting against
dead religion, against empty rules and regulations,
against the powerful keeping down the powerless,
against a minority controlling the wealth, against . . .
well, tons of stuff. And, as the liberation theologians
have pointed out, in some ways, in some places
following Jesus may mean a revolution against the
prevailing powers that be, the rulers of darkness, the
principalities and powers, corrupt regimes and
dodgy dictators.
So, part one of this saying – "Come the

THE REVOLUTION

Revolution" – yes, Jesus was up for that. Part two, well, dubious really. That's the trouble with Jesus, you can't fit him in with any prevailing political trend or orthodoxy. Yeah, we'll have a revolution, but we won't torture and kill the baddies – we'll forgive them and pray that love will regenerate them so that they have their own place in the new order, so that they're part of the new community. This approach annoys many revolutionaries – it's too awkward, confusing and slows the process down quite a bit. A political opposition is much easier to deal with if they're in the graveyard. Still that's the thing with Jesus, it's (watch out reader, very dodgy-sixties-vibe about to make an appearance in a kaftan) a Revolution of Love. (Baby!)

146

Charity begins at home.
This is a phrase used by Christians and non-believers alike to give legitimacy to gross and repulsive selfishness. Under its supposedly noble banner, vast sums are spent on Little Johnny's education, to give him the "best start in life"; vast sums are spent on buying a house with a large garden so Little Johnny has space to play; and vast sums are spent on over-priced toys to buy Little Johnny love. Little Johnny

CHARITY

also needs a freezer filled by Marks and Spencer's, and rather expensive foreign holidays. Of course he does. And all this self-indulgence in the name of "charity". Marvellous. Let's hope Jesus never said anything like, "My mother and brothers are those who hear the word of God and obey it." That would really spoil the party.

147

And pigs will fly!
A prophetic word from Jesus concerning the twentieth-century police use of helicopters.

148

Religion is the opium of the people.
Thank you Karl Marx. And goodnight.

149

I realize now I handled things all wrong with the Romans and the Jewish authorities. Given another chance I would have approached them on their own level, not going for so much confrontation, and trying harder to avoid misunderstanding. I think if

FLYING PIGS

I'd done that I would have been able to gain their respect – naturally this would have entailed a certain weakening of my message, certain compromises, but these no doubt would have resulted in certain advantages too. For example, I wouldn't have been killed. This of course introduces the problem of if I had not been killed then neither could I be raised from the dead. To some this would have been a weakening of my message – however to others it would have been seen as a greater approachability, more identification with the people of the time. I think I would have been more circumspect too about my identity. When one reveals that one truly is the Son of God this tends to go down rather badly in polite company. I wouldn't do that again. Then there was the business of the virgin birth. People have never forgotten it – that's true – but, did they ever really understand what it meant? I'm not so sure.

<u>150</u>

Faith in God is about your personal life, not about social and political issues. I know it's tough out there but look, in Heaven everything will be fine. Honest, just you wait and see, or better still, wait and pray. But, please, no action.

HEAVEN

Blessed are the warmongers.
Ring any bells? No. Perhaps you're thinking of
"Blessed are the peacemakers". . . .

152

*My mother-in-law, I'm not saying she's fat but when
she falls over she rocks herself to sleep trying to get
up. She was lying in the road once as I approached
in the car. It wasn't that I couldn't have driven
round her. It was just that I didn't have enough
petrol. No – seriously though, my mother-in-law,
she's a wonderful woman – so soft and tender. Just
like a cold sore. And I'm not joking when I say I do
have a very soft spot for her. Yes, some quicksands
near Dover . . .*

Jesus never had a Mother-in-law, although he *knew*
one. After all, he healed Peter's from illness – after
which, she gave them all a great meal. But Jesus
wasn't into mother-in-law jokes, or indeed, any
jokes about women. He made plenty of rude
comments, of course. But interestingly, never about
women. His figures of fun tended to be male and
powerful – priests, Levites, stupid builders, rich
men who didn't notice others, etc, etc. Nothing

MOTHER-IN-LAWS

about mothers-in-law. This, I suppose, made him the first alternative comedian. And maybe the last one too. After all, he must be the only alternative comedian who's never done a lager advert. Very alternative, lager adverts, eh? About as prophetic as Des O'Connor.

153

There's No Such Thing as Society . . .
Well, she was spiritual leader to millions but in fact the words of Mrs Margaret Thatcher often, as in this case, departed radically from those of our Lord. He was very big on stuff like "community" – you know, twelve disciples, talk about sharing one another's burdens and this sort of thing. 'Course, he lived before people had thought of the word "individualism" but he wouldn't have been a fan of it. Not that he was against a bit of solitary – he often wandered off for days to pray – but he believed people were made to be together, in families, in homes, in synagogues, in churches, in football teams, even in each other's pockets – the disciples had a shared purse. The faith Jesus illustrated was a social faith where everybody is invited – a Christian society where even people who don't believe in society are welcome.

MARGARET THATCHER

154

*When you pray, say this: God bless Mum, Dad,
Granny (if she's still alive) and Bluey the Budgie.
Also, see to my friend Jerry, 'cos today he nicked my
toffo/parking space/wife. But most of all, bless me
and my schemes.*

Prayer is not asking God to "baptize" things as they
are; prayer isn't an attempt to make sure the tide of
life continues to flow your way. It isn't a way of
organizing the external events in your life, so they
suit you better.

Rather, prayer is opening yourself to the possibility
of a Mysterious "Other", who is trying to speak with
you; prayer is meeting with the living Jesus and
watching, listening, asking. Prayer is being taken
out of yourself, however momentarily, and becoming
absorbed with the Divine.

155

A Mars a Day Helps you work, rest and pray.
Get your ears tested.

MARS BARS

156

A Quiet Time every day keeps the Devil away.
If only 'twas so simple.

157

If only I'd known that I'd have to sit for thousands of years and listen to the same Lord's Prayer repeated mindlessly in thousands of school assemblies – I'd never have taught it in the first place! Thank goodness I only bothered with the short version.

158

Peter, I wonder if I could give you half a dozen items for your prayer list?

159

Love is never having to say you're sorry . . .
Tosh from the film *Love Story*, in fact.

PRAYER LISTS

160

*Read, Mark, Learn. And while he's at it, the same
goes for you, Peter, James, John. . . .*

161

Have you Tried These Little Notes of Mine, Every
Day With Me?

162

A chapter a day, keeps insomnia at bay.
If you're not too careful.

163

*Did you like my biography? It has had mixed
reviews. I think I prefer some of the movies instead,
to be completely honest. I'm a little concerned that
no one much reads it these days – though it has
lasted quite some time. In fact I'm looking for
someone to revise it radically – taking out some of
the more difficult and boring bits and spicing up the
thing generally. I'm being put under a great deal*

of pressure to get sales back up to where they were a few hundred years ago. You may be able to answer a question that has been puzzling me for some time now: Why is it that it says inside the front cover of every edition of the Bible that it is illegal to read it out loud in public? It seems these copyright chaps have got a bit ahead of themselves on that one.

164

Thaddaeus, how's your memorizing of Leviticus coming on . . . ? And James, how are you getting on with Second Chronicles? Let's try chapter 3 verses 11 to 17, shall we?

165

Take this book with you and carry it on your person wherever you may travel. When darkness comes, when trouble threatens, when sin closes in and it seems there is no way out . . . pull it out and, with a deep breath and the faintest hint of a prayer, flick it open at random. I think you'll find it does the trick most times. . . .
Warning: This is not an infallible method: We know

THE BIBLE

someone who once, feeling particularly depressed,
adopted this usually excellent advice. With his first
random flick-search his finger alighted on the verse,
"Judas went out and hanged himself. . . ."
Looking for something just a touch more positive,
he tried a second time and found his finger
highlighting further wise instruction, *"Go and do
thou likewise. . . ."*

166

*Matthew, I hope I didn't see you reading a copy of
that dodgy modern Testament earlier. I thought I'd
made it clear . . . the King James Version is the one
I recommend. It's the one Moses used after all . . .
and I've got some very good bulk-order discounts on
it.*

167

Repaint, Repaint – and thin no more.
These famous words of Jesus were originally said to
Jereboam, a dodgy painter and decorator from
Capernaum, after our Lord caught him watering
down the paint, whilst working on Martha's front
room.

THE GOOD BOOK

168

Evangelists do it in tents.
Actually, they usually do it just about anywhere.
They simply can't keep a lid on it.

169

Tell 'em what they want to hear – that's my motto!
Jesus in fact spent a lot of his time telling people
exactly the opposite of what they wanted to hear.
Stuff about humility, forgiveness, purity of motive,
service of others – all in all, he gave the furtive
human soul no quarter. The last straw was him
telling anyone who wanted to follow him to
shoulder the gallows beam. Just what everyone
wanted to hear, that. No wonder he died friendless
apart from a few resilient women. . . .

170

*The 1990s, yes, I think that might be a good decade
for some evangelism.*
Er, well, he didn't actually say this, or not while he
was around bodily, if you see what we mean. But
some people think he told them later, spiritually,

EVANGELISM

around about the late 1980s actually. Trouble is, unless God has a lisp or an exaggerated problem with pronunciation or some kind of stutter, then his listeners must have a problem in hearing him. While the evangelicals all thought he said, "I decree there should be a Decade of *Evangelism* in the 1990s", the Roman Catholics all thought he said, "Decade of *Evangelization*". This has led some to suggest that maybe we could do with a *Decade of Pronunciation* or a *Decade of Clarification of Our Terms* first. Or at least a *Decade of Listening to Each Other Before We Start Talking to Everyone Else.*

171

Life is no laughing matter. I'm basically a man of sorrows when it comes down to it.

172

A vote for me is a vote for a better standard of living. . . .
Jesus never stood in any election. If he had he would probably have promised a worse standard of living. And, of course, he would have lost. Despite this people have elected for him ever since.

LIFE

173

God never got a joke in his eternal life.

174

Just look up, cheer up, and keep smiling,
You'll be caught up to glory someday!

175

God takes the best ones first.

This profound comment by Jesus explains why so many children have died in the history of the world through disease, famine, gun-fire and neglect. That was God "taking the best ones first" – doing them a huge favour. So amidst the pleading screams we can comfort ourselves with the thought that it's just God going about his business of lavishing love on his favourites, "the best ones". The logic of this comment, of course, also asks us to look again at the survivors. Those who haven't been taken. Those who must, by definition, be the worst ones on God's scorecard. The dregs, the scum, whom God frankly finds rather repulsive. Should we really therefore be throwing good money after bad by paying out

SMILING

pensions to OAPs? If they were anything half-decent,
they'd have been taken years ago. . . .

176

Time's A great Healer.
Wrong. Time doesn't heal. It merely numbs,
obscures, blurs, dims. There's only one healer.
Love.

177

*I'm going to spend the first million years of eternity
getting to the heart of painting.*
Nice idea. But Winston Churchill said it.

178

*Why is it that people think that after death there is
The Big Nothing? Is it because when they ask dead
people where they've gone they just say nothing?*

179

Ideas have Consequences.
Jesus didn't say this because, even though it's true,
it sounds so anaesthetizingly boring that it ought to
be credited to no one.

WINSTON CHURCHILL

180

I love religion. Religion, believe it or not, was the best idea I could come up with in the time available (eternity) in the absence of the Saatchi Bros. My purpose was to get across to the target audience the idea that I am a liberty-loving kinda guy (who isn't simply a guy, but no need to do any sexual/theological jumping-to-conclusions-here) who just wanted to have fun, and so stopped off between one thing and another to create a new planet and some new friends to play with. Well! How was I to know that I'd have been better off waiting a few hundred thousand years to see how the Conservative Party managed to sell something much worse much better. I was assured endlessly at the time that religion was a sure-fire hit.

181

Do have a think about what I'm telling you – and any other religious teachers you come across for that matter. . . .It's not binding, don't let it oppress you, but there just might be something in it for you to chew on. Eh?
Occasionally a religious leader will come along who tells his slightly stunned followers that his

RELIGION

suggestions are only that, his advice merely advisory and his comments open to debate. Not *that* occasionally though, and Jesus was like most other religious leaders in that respect. He wasn't offering blessed morning reflections for Radio Four listeners to mull on. He was, awkward as it seems in these tolerant times, rather bolshie with his views. You know, stuff about hell, about the last judgement, about when did you see me naked, hungry, thirsty, about our wealth blocking up the needle-eye entrance into the Kingdom, about selling all you have and giving to the poor . . . it goes on. Not least he was rather emphatic about himself. Hard to recall the last contributor to *Thought for the Day* who concluded his comments by revealing to listeners that he was in fact in his very person the path to salvation, the answer to their questions, the light in their darkness, er, and so on. Jesus wouldn't have been allowed on the programme, his script would have been radically amended or turned down flat.
Ooh, er, Missus.

182

What does it matter what you believe? God understands and believes in you. . . .
Yes, true, God does believe in us. Odd when you

GOD

think how unbelievable we are. After all, he is much more believable than we are.

183

Stupid are those who know they are spiritually poor. . . .
I mean, they have just got to be the worst party-poopers imaginable.
Stupid are those who mourn . . .
Hey look, cheer up, all right?! It might never happen!
Stupid are the meek. . . .
To be blunt, you've got to sell yourself, kid. That's the way it is.
Stupid are those whose greatest desire is to do what God requires. . . .
Life's too short frankly to get into that heavy stuff.
Stupid are those who show mercy to others. . . .
For they shall be called "Mugs". Right? RIGHT!
Stupid are the pure in heart. . . .
Leave all that nonsense to what's-her-face? Mother Teresa, yeah.
And the other guy. No, not Cliff Richard. The one with the ring 'n' robes. The Pope, yeah. Him.
Stupid are those who work for peace. . . .

NOT THE BEATITUDES

And pretty depressed too! 'cos basically the whole
shebang has been, and will be, war from beginning
to end.
And, stupid are those who suffer persecution because
they do what God requires. . . .
No, I mean, I respect them in a way. Very worthy
and all that.
But, I mean, it's no life is it?
So to sum up, let's go surfin', eh?

184

You're all going to burn in Hell!
Commonly believed, by many preachers of the more
fundamentalist and foaming-at-the-mouth variety,
to be an incentive to the audience to listen in to
what they have to say to them about their eternal
destiny. In fact market research indicates that it
annoys people quite a bit and tends to make them
think, "Get stuffed, you arrogant, dog-collared
plonker" rather than the more helpful, "Come
again, Rev, what you trying to lay on me there?"
All the textual critics suggest that while Jesus made
frequent reference to Hell, the after-life, Hades,
the place of the dead and other related subject-
matter, he never actually consigned anyone to the

HELL

place in question at any given moment. On the other hand, he did tell a common-or-garden thief, specializing in rather annoying nocturnal car-stereo removals, that despite the present predicament – hanging by his nails six feet off the ground – his own small faith would guarantee their renewed acquaintance later that day in paradise. Interesting that.

185

Sincerity is the key – as long as you're sincere, eh? "That's what I said, too." (A. Hitler)

186

DISCIPLE: Jesus. . . ?

JESUS: *Yes.*

DISCIPLE: I've been thinking about what you said about going into all the world, like. . . .

JESUS: *Yes.*

DISCIPLE: . . . to preach the Gospel, you know, to the ends of the earth, like.

JESUS: *Yes.*

DISCIPLE: Well, it seems a bit ambitious.

SINCERITY

JESUS: *Ah, that's because we haven't got around to talking about our target audience yet.*

DISCIPLE: Oh.

JESUS: *Yes, we're going to have to target our message very carefully. But we can't do that until we've undertaken our market research into what people are keen to hear about, what kind of message they might be receptive to.*

DISCIPLE: Oh.

JESUS: *Having established that, we'll then need to work on our product – exactly what kind of message we want to get across to the people – for example, what doctrines we should bother with and what ones we won't stand a chance with – and then we begin the marketing.*

DISCIPLE: Marketing?

JESUS: *Yes, billboards, poster-campaigns, television advertising, electronic display boards in the Temple Courts, sponsoring windsurfers on the Sea of Galilee . . . all that sort of thing.*

DISCIPLE: Sounds a bit complicated all that.

JESUS: *Ah yes, but it's a lot more effective in getting a real presence in public perceptions, in raising our corporate profile, than, say, chatting with lepers in backstreets or visiting people with AIDS.*

DISCIPLE: Right. . . .

MARKETING

187

I say unto you that The Holy Father is Unholy, that the Pope is the anti-Me.

And if you think that sounds more like the Rev. Ian Paisley than Jesus, you'd be dead right. Except Rev. Paisley calls the Pope the anti-Christ, not the anti-Me, because Rev. Paisley may have started his own denomination but he doesn't claim to be the Christ.

188

In an emergency, call in your nearest doctrine.

189

What I like about religion is all the rules and regulations.

Actually, this is what he mainly didn't like. Which is why the people who did soon ruled and regulated his life away.

190

Why should the Devil have all the good music?
Well, he's used to it by now.

THE DEVIL

*When I was on earth I was a little rushed for time
and didn't get a real chance to fill you in on the
things that Heaven has to offer, or for that matter
hell. On one occasion I did start to tell the guys
about it but I got distracted by a leper. Anyway, in
my Father's house there are many mansions and
each one is built in a rather attractive neo-Tudor
style with beams, triple glazing throughout, leather
suites from Kingdom of Leather, oak veneer country-
style fully-fitted kitchens, en-suite bathrooms with
lo-level furniture, and triple garages with one of
those things that opens the garage doors for you
without you having to get out of your car. . . . I think
you'll like it. Am I tempting you?
The Other Place has certain similarities – there are
many mansions and each one is built in a rather
attractive neo-Tudor style with beams, triple glazing
throughout, leather suites from Kingdom of
Leather, oak veneer country-style fully-fitted
kitchens, en-suite bathrooms with lo-level furniture,
and triple garages with one of those things that opens
the garage doors for you without you having to get
out of the car. . . . I think you'll like it if you've got
your heart set on that kind of thing.*

HEAVEN

An Englishman is a self-made man who worships his own creator.

Jesus would probably have said this had he got around to visiting.

193

You can never be too sure about foreigners. That's my view anyway, stick to your own kind, eh? Take those Samaritans, for example, now they can be a real pain in the butt.

An extra-terrestrial theologian might deduce such words from the founder of Christianity if all he had to go on was the behaviour of his followers, the Church, down the centuries. Christians don't have too clever a record on treating everyone equally. It took rather a long time before slavery was abolished, by a Christian called Wilberforce actually, but even longer for less obvious things like discrimination against people of other colours or of a different sex to be fixed – in fact it isn't done yet. Many churches think only humans in possession of the male member – which unfortunately rules out most female Christians – can be ordained to the priesthood.

FOREIGNERS

Some commentators argue that it was the Church's attitude to Jewish people down the centuries that eventually gave rise to Hitler and the Holocaust. And it was only recently that the Dutch Reformed Church in South Africa decided that perhaps having a black skin didn't make you less of a person in the sight of God than someone with a white skin, and agreed that maybe their long-standing, er, theological basis to apartheid was stretching the Good Book a touch too far.

Makes you wonder where these people picked up their ideas about Jesus. Seems a million miles away from the one who had girls for best friends and told stories about banquets for beggars and good Samaritans.

194

Enjoy life. This is not a rehearsal.
No. It is a rehearsal. That's exactly what it is. It must be. No one seems to have got their act together yet.

LIFE

God is an Englishman . . . about 6ft 1in with blond hair and blue-grey eyes. His suits are made in Savile Row – he favours his jackets with a single vent, and he has always worn turn-ups. Shirts with a starched detachable collar is what he wears most of the time, from Turnbull and Asser, though I can secretly reveal that he has experimented from time to time with fixed collars. He always wears gold cufflinks, but nothing flashy. Ties are always silk but not florid or camp. God prefers to wear braces not a belt. These days he tends not to wear a hat though he did quite a bit in the past – but you might well catch him in a Panama on a Saturday in the garden. He has never worn a pair of jeans in his life. He has had his hair cut once a fortnight at the same place in Curzon Street for the last forty years. If it looks like rain you'll find him wearing a waxed cotton jacket, but he feels these are becoming a little too common in town nowadays.

GOD'S ENGLISH PERIOD

197

The Gods may throw the dice
Their minds as cold as ice
And someone way down here
Loses someone dear.

Irony of ironies. That ABBA, that most treasured of
all pop groups, should so misunderstand the other
ABBA, the one described by Jesus. Still, a great
tune, Bjorn. Love the tune.

198

One's nearer to God in the garden than anywhere
else on earth.
Yes, of course one is. The fact that the Bible records
such a disappointing start to things in a garden
(Genesis) and yet such a brilliant finish to things in
a city (Revelation), must be a, er, printing error.

199

Whatever will be, will be.
Unless anyone's got any better ideas.

ABBA

Call me old-fashioned.
No. Jesus was never in fashion. He didn't fit in first-century Palestine. He didn't fit in the tomb. He hasn't fitted in ever since. He is a fashion disaster, lovey – total disaster.

.................Here Endeth The Lessons ....

THE END IS NIGH

THE END HAS JUST NIGHED